# WE CELEBRATE CINCO DE MAYO IN SPRING

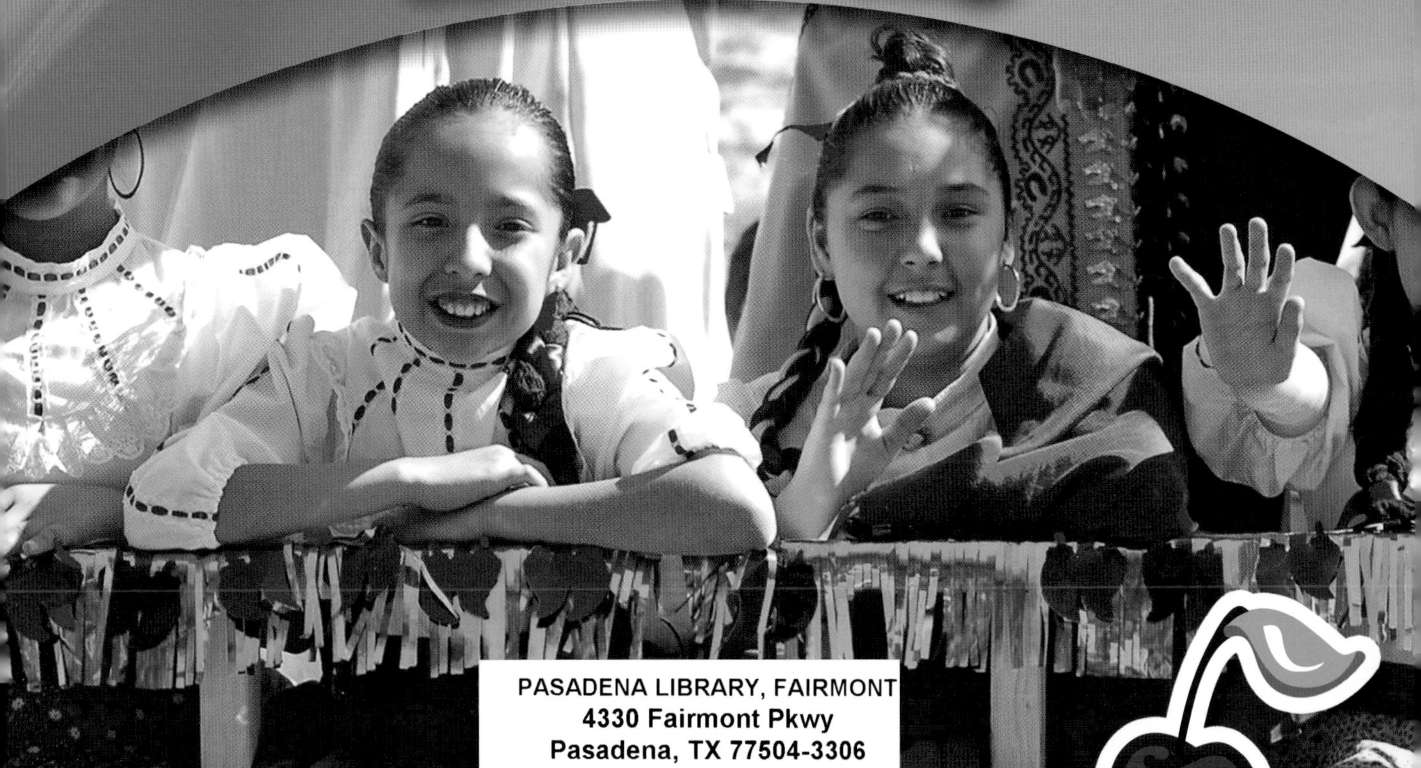

1

by Jenna Lee Gleisner

Cherry Lake Publishing • Ann Arbor, Michigan

Published in the United States of America
by Cherry Lake Publishing
Ann Arbor, Michigan
www.cherrylakepublishing.com

Consultant: Marla Conn, ReadAbility, Inc.

Photo Credits: Shutterstock Images, Cover, Title; Vaclav Volrab/Shutterstock Images, 4; Faraways/Shutterstock Images, 6; Richard Levine/age fotostock/SuperStock, 8; Tom Wang/Shutterstock Images, 10; Stanislaw Tokarski/Shutterstock Images, 12; Joshua Resnick/Shutterstock Images, 14; David Kay/Shutterstock Images, 16; White House, 18; Thinkstock, 20



Library of Congress Cataloging-in-Publication Data
Gleisner, Jenna Lee.
We celebrate Cinco de Mayo in spring / by Jenna Lee Gleisner.
pages cm. -- (Let's look at spring)
Audience: 5-7.
Audience: K to grade 3.
Includes index.
ISBN 978-1-62431-657-9 (hardcover) -- ISBN 978-1-62431-684-5 (pbk.) -- ISBN 978-1-62431-711-8 (pdf) -- ISBN 978-1-62431-738-5 (hosted ebook)
1. Cinco de Mayo (Mexican holiday)--Juvenile literature. I. Title.

F1233.G54 2014
394.262--dc23

2013028941

Cherry Lake Publishing would like to acknowledge the work of The Partnership for 21st Century Skills. Please visit *www.p21.org* for more information.

Printed in the United States of America
Corporate Graphics Inc.
January 2014

# TABLE OF CONTENTS

# Spring Begins

Spring is here. It gets warmer.
It is time for a fun holiday.

Cinco de Mayo is Spanish. It means "fifth of May." It is on May 5.

## What Do You See?

How many girls are dancing?

# Celebrate

We **celebrate** this holiday in the United States. Some people in Mexico do, too.

We celebrate Mexican **culture**. Kim learns about a big **battle** in Mexico on this day.

# Fun Parties

We watch parades. Bands play lively music. People dance and laugh.

## What Do You See?

What toppings does Mya's mom put on the tacos?

Mya's mom cooks tacos. Her family enjoys the holiday together.

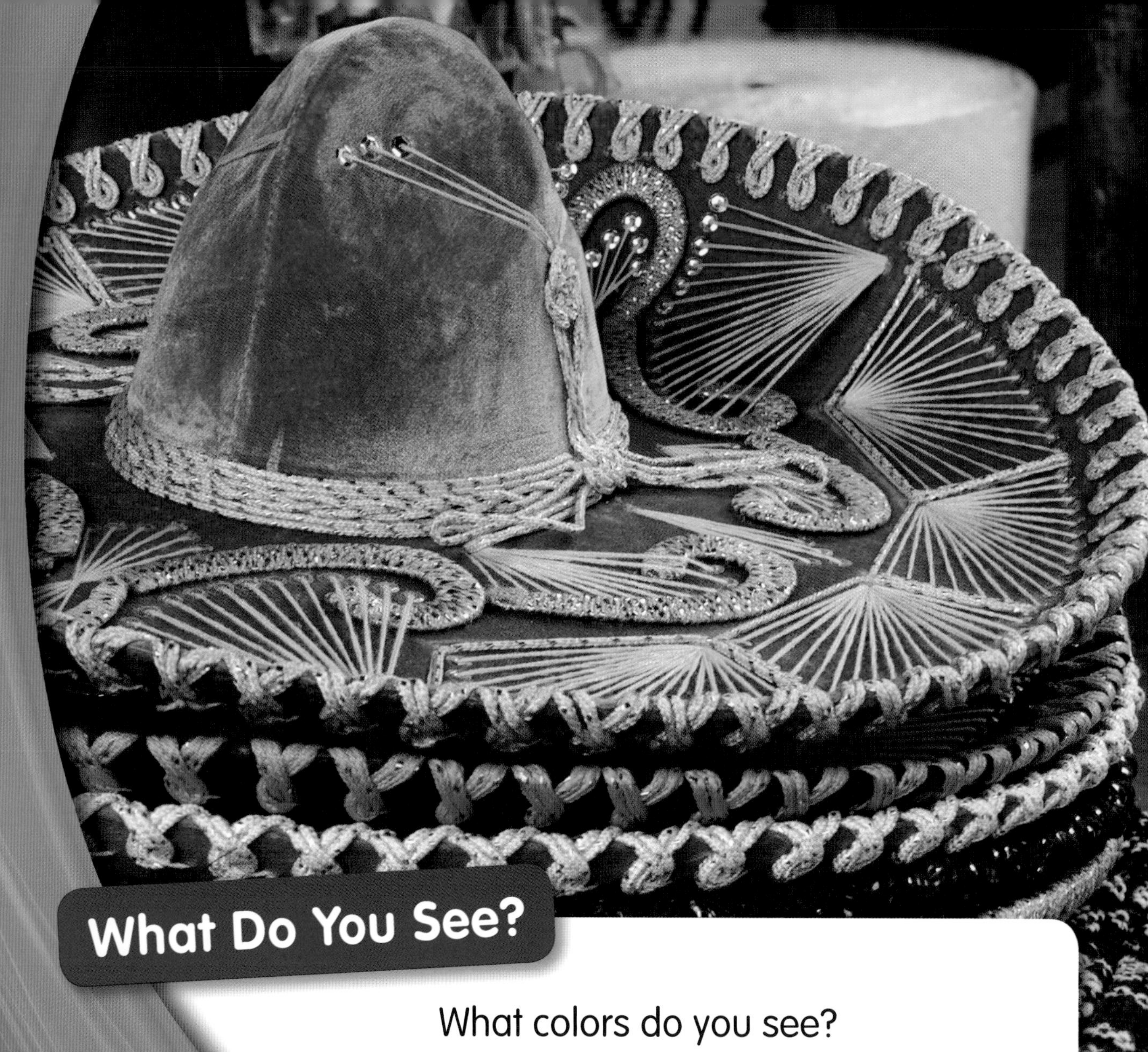

## What Do You See?

What colors do you see?

# Dress Up

People dress up. They wear **sombreros**.

Rosa wears a long dress. It has the colors of Mexico's flag.

How do you celebrate Cinco de Mayo?

# Find Out More

## BOOK

Hall, M. C. *Cinco de Mayo*. Vero Beach, FL: Rourke Publishing, 2011.

## WEB SITE

**History—Cinco de Mayo**

*www.history.com/topics/cinco-de-mayo/videos#cinco-de-mayo*

Watch a video to learn more about why we celebrate Cinco de Mayo.

# Glossary

**battle** (BAT-uhl) a fight between two armies

**celebrate** (SEL-uh-brate) to enjoy an event or holiday with others

**culture** (KUHL-chur) a group's ideas and ways of life

**sombrero** (sahm-BRAIR-oh) a tall and wide hat

# Home and School Connection

Use this list of words from the book to help your child become a better reader. Word games and writing activities can help beginning readers reinforce literacy skills.

bands
battle
big
celebrate
colors
cooks
culture
dance
dress
family
flag
fun
holiday
laugh
learns
lively
long
May
music
parades
people
play
sombrero
Spanish
spring
tacos
warmer
watch

## What Do You See?

What Do You See? is a feature paired with select photos in this book. It encourages young readers to interact with visual images in order to build the ability to integrate content in various media formats.

You can help your child further evaluate photos in this book with additional activities. Look at the images in the book without the What Do You See? feature. Ask your child to point out one detail in each image, such as a color, time of day, animal, or setting.

# Index



# About the Author

Jenna Lee Gleisner is an editor and author who lives in Minnesota. She celebrates Cinco de Mayo by eating lots of Mexican food!